COOL PETS for Kids

Birds

DAWN TITMUS

PowerKiDS press

Published in 2019 by The Rosen
Publishing Group, Inc.
29 East 21st Street, New York, NY 10010

Cataloging-in-Publication Data

Names: Titmus, Dawn.
Title: Birds / Dawn Titmus.
Description: New York : PowerKids Press, 2019. | Series: Cool pets for kids | Includes glossary and index
Identifiers: LCCN ISBN 9781538338636 (pbk.) | ISBN 9781538338629 (library bound) |
ISBN 9781538338643 (6 pack)
Subjects: LCSH: Cage birds--Juvenile literature. | Birds -- Juvenile literature. | Birds as pets.
Classification: LCC SF461.35 T58 2019 | DDC 636.6˙8--dc23

Text and editor: Dawn Titmus
Editorial Director: Lindsey Lowe
Children's Publisher: Anne O'Daly
Design Manager: Keith Davis
Picture Manager: Sophie Mortimer

Photo acknowledgements:
t=top, c=center, b=bottom, l=left, r=right
Interior: Alamy: Angela Hampton Picture Library 25b, blickwinkel/foto 11b, Blue Jean Images 7t, Juniors
Bildarchiv GmbH 23t; Amazon: Trixie Pet Products 13b; Dreamstime: cynoclub 22–23, Brian Lansenby
10–11t; iStock: Brosa 14, CasPhotography 25t, GlobalIP 4-5, Leopardinatree 19t, Lusyaya 21t, Multiart 6–7,
Nickbeer 12b, pchoul 18b, tucko019 7bl, 7br, tunart 1, vitalssss 8, vitcom 10, Yobra10 15b; Shutterstock:
BestPhotoStudio 15t, Butterfly Hunter 26–27, Coldmoon Photoproject 10–11c, cynoclub 20–21, GaevoyB
23b, giftkie 29t, Glass and Nature 29b, guentermanaus 29c, Eric Isselee 12–13, 24–25, Kolonko 20, 22, 24, 26,
Wang LiQiang 27t, Lucky Business 17, Tanya Morozz 12t, nattanan726 19b, photomaster 16–17, Saman527 9b,
santypan 16, Theodore Scott 27b, Elena Shutlova 9t, Tracey Starr 3, Santhosh Varghese 5, 21b, Olga Vasilyeva
4, Daniel Zuppinger 18t.

Manufactured in the United States of America

CPSIA Compliance Information: Batch #CSPK18: For Further Information contact Rosen Publishing, New York,
New York at 1-800-237-9932.

Contents

Which Bird?

Birds are fascinating, intelligent creatures and looking after a bird can be great fun, but choose your pet carefully. All birds need care and attention, and some are more demanding than others.

Your Home and Lifestyle

Before you choose a bird, think about how much time and space you have. Parrots like attention. Canaries are happy to be left alone in their cage. Some birds need more space than others. A small bird such as a budgerigar is a good choice if you live in an apartment. A larger bird such as a macaw needs a big cage and time to fly outside it. The cage needs to be big enough for your pet to be able to move around easily.

Healthy Bird

It is important to choose a healthy bird. The eyes should be bright and clear, and there should be no bald patches in the feathers. Pet birds need yearly checkups at the vet.

Adopt a Bird

Before you buy a bird, see if you can adopt one from your local animal shelter or an avian rescue organization. Avian vets, who specialize in birds, often know of birds in need of homes. You could also check the advertisements in the local paper or pet store.

The Right Bird for You?

☑ Do you have time to look after a bird?

☑ Do you have the space for a bird and its cage?

☑ Are you able to provide your bird with food and water every day?

☑ Can you make your home a safe place for a bird?

☑ Will you take your bird to the vet regularly?

☑ Do you have other pets such as a dog or cat?

Read On ...

Birds are wonderful pets, but it is important to choose the right one. This book will help you pick and care for your pet. Learn about four types of birds that are popular as pets. Try your hand at making tasty bird treats. You will also find some fascinating facts about our feathery friends!

What You Will Need

All pet birds need some basic items, such as food and water containers, a birdbath, and some toys. The biggest and most important item is the cage, where your bird will spend most of its time.

What You Need

- ☑ A cage big enough for your bird's needs.
- ☑ Perches for the cage.
- ☑ Food and water containers.
- ☑ Toys such as ladders and puzzles.
- ☑ Birdbath.
- ☑ Bird-safe cleaner.

Playtime

Giving your bird toys to play with will help prevent boredom. Change the toys in the cage frequently for more variety. Try toys that your bird can use for foraging or shredding. You can find these in pet stores or you can make your own. Your bird will also enjoy a birdbath that can be clipped on to the side of the cage.

Toys keep birds entertained.

The Cage

Decide where in the home you want the bird to live. It is best not to put a cage in the kitchen, as cooking fumes could harm your bird. Keep the cage away from windows, too. The sun could cause your bird to overheat. The best place is next to a wall in a room where you spend a lot of time.

Perches

Perches encourage your bird to exercise. Changing the position of the perches in the cage makes life more interesting for your pet. You can use well-scrubbed branches to make your own perches from non-poisonous trees such as sycamore and apple.

Food and Water

Most cages have covered food and water containers that clip to the side of the cage. Your bird may bathe or leave droppings in an open water container. Most cages have a floor that slides out for easy cleaning. Remove food and droppings from the floor every day.

Water container

Food container

Feeding Time

Your bird needs the right amount of food every day to keep it fit and healthy. It also needs a supply of clean water. What kind of food your bird needs depends on its type.

Bird Food

Feed your bird a balanced diet with quality pellets (dried food) and a variety of fresh fruits, vegetables, and grains. Birdseed does not contain all the nutrients a bird needs, but it is a good snack. Make sure you get the right mix for your bird. Millet sprays are nutritious.Cuttlebones provide calcium. Chewing on them helps birds keep their beak in trim.

Egg Food

Egg food is full of protein and vitamins that your bird needs. You can buy it from the pet-supply store. Or you can make your own with hardboiled egg yolks and chopped-up dandelion leaves.

Wild Plants

Parrots and finches eat wild plants such as chickweed and dandelions. If these grow in your yard, make sure they haven't been sprayed with chemicals before giving them to your pet.

Dandelion

Tasty Treats

Green leafy vegetables, such as mustard greens, chard, and spinach, can be added to your pet's diet. Most birds also like bell peppers, corn (right), and carrots, and fruits such as bananas, melons, and grapes. Make sure the food is washed and cut into small pieces before feeding it to your pet.

Watch Out!

There are some foods that are harmful to birds. Dairy products such as milk and cheese can cause an upset stomach. Foods such as chocolate, avocados, rhubarb leaves, and onions can make birds sick.

Millet spray

Grooming and Cleaning

In the wild, birds take care of their own grooming. Caged birds don't need grooming as much as some other pets, such as dogs, but they may need some help.

Bath Time

Many birds will use a birdbath to keep themselves clean. Some parrots like a fine water spray. A houseplant sprayer is good for this. Fill it with clean, tepid water. Hold it up and away from the bird so the spray falls onto it from above like fine raindrops. Do not spray directly into the bird's face.

Birdbath

Claws and Beaks

In the wild, a bird's claws wear down naturally. A caged bird may have overgrown claws that need to be trimmed. Claws have a blood supply, so it important to cut off only the sharp, pointed tip. Beaks may also need to be trimmed, particularly in parakeets. It is best to ask the vet to trim the claws and beak.

Neat Feathers

Birds use their beak to comb their feathers. This keeps them clean and removes parasites. Birds also arrange the strands of their feathers so they are lying flat. Birds preen themselves like this several times a day.

Keeping Clean

Clean your bird's cage, toys, and containers regularly. This will help keep your pet healthy. Be sure to use a cleaning product that is bird safe—some can harm birds. After cleaning, rinse everything in clean water.

Exercise

Birds like to fly! If there is little space for your bird to fly in its cage, let it spend some time outside the cage. Make sure your home is bird proof first.

Settling In

Allow your bird to settle in for a few days when you first bring it home. When it is settled, you can try coaxing it out of its cage. Open the cage door and offer your pet a treat. Allow it to come out at its own pace. Do not try to handle your pet, as it will get scared. Leave the door open so it can come and go when it wants.

Perching

Your bird will want to perch on things when it is out of the cage. Make sure some furniture in the room is suitable for perching. A special bird T-stand (stand in the shape of a T) is ideal.

Flying Time

The chance for your bird to fly is good exercise and a boredom buster. Close all windows and doors to prevent your bird escaping. Also pull the drapes and close the blinds so your bird does not fly into windows. Make sure any other pets, such as cats and dogs, are safely away in another room. Birds like to chew, so put any wires, cords, or other chewable items out of sight. Turn off any heaters, ceiling fans, and other appliances.

More Space

If you have space in your yard, you could consider a flight cage or a small aviary. You can buy kits to put together that don't take up much space. Position the aviary so that it is out of the wind and will be in the shade for part of the day.

Training

Birds are intelligent, and many of them can be taught to do tricks. Some birds can be trained to talk! Give your bird plenty of toys and play with it every day to prevent boredom.

Tricks and Treats

Parrots and parakeets are especially good at learning tricks. You could train your bird to turn around, wave, dance, or jump. Use treats as rewards when your bird does what you want it to do.

Ignore the Bad

Ignore the behavior you do not want. Never yell at your bird or punish it. Birds can become aggressive and bite if they are scared. You could try distracting your bird from bad behavior. If your bird screams when its food bowls are being filled, give it a toy or snack to keep it busy.

Finger Tame

Some birds become so tame they will happily sit on your finger. You can encourage your pet to step onto your hand. Carefully place your hand inside the cage alongside the perch. Some birds may find it scary to have a hand in their cage, so go slowly. If your bird steps onto your fingers, reward it with a treat such as a piece of apple.

Talking Time

Some birds such as parrots and budgerigars can be taught to talk. Try singing to your bird and copying the sounds it makes. Keep repeating the words you want your bird to say. Keep the training sessions short. A few minutes several times a day is better than a long session. Training a bird to talk takes a lot of patience. Don't be disappointed if your bird doesn't talk back to you immediately!

Staying Healthy

You can help your bird stay healthy by giving it the right food and clean water every day. Also make sure it gets enough exercise and has plenty of toys. Even so, birds get sick sometimes, just like humans.

Signs of Sickness

A bird can show it is not feeling well in several ways:

- ✔ It is not thirsty or hungry.
- ✔ It seems tired or less active than usual.
- ✔ It sits hunched over, with its feathers fluffed up.
- ✔ Its eyes are dull or closed.
- ✔ It sleeps on both legs rather than just on one leg.
- ✔ It is sneezing or has a runny nose.
- ✔ Its droppings look different from normal.

Take your bird to the vet straight away if you think it is ill.

Yearly Checkups

Take your bird to the vet when you first get it. Also take it once a year for a checkup. Your vet will check your bird's weight and ask questions about your pet's general health. It is best to find a specialist avian vet if you can.

Keeping Clean

If your bird has been ill, it's important to clean the cage and food and water containers to prevent disease from spreading. Also be sure to wash your hands every time you handle a sick bird.

Common Problems

Birds can develop problems with their claws, beak, and feathers. Claws can get too long and make perching difficult. The beak may also grow too long. Birds use their beak for grooming, eating, and balance. An overlong beak can make these behaviors difficult. The vet can help with claw and beak trimmings. Birds may pluck their feathers. There are many reasons for feather plucking, such as sickness, boredom, or a poor diet. Take your bird to the vet for advice if it starts to pluck out its feathers.

In the Wild

Finches, parrots, and softbills such as toucans are among the most popular birds to keep as pets. Cage birds are bred in captivity, but they often show the same behavior as birds in the wild.

Singing Birds

In the wild, many birds defend their territory and attract a mate by singing. People keep canaries and the singing finches because of their beautiful song.

Eating Habits

Birds in the wild eat food that keeps them fit and healthy. For example, Toucans eat mainly fruit. It is important to feed your bird the type of food it would find and eat in the wild.

Finding a Mate

Many types of parrots mate for life. Both parents look after the eggs until they hatch and care for the young birds. In finches, only the female bird looks after the eggs and young birds. Some birds, such as lovebirds, are happier as pets if they have a companion to live with. Pairs of lovebirds will play with and groom one another.

Living in Flocks

Parrots are social birds. In the wild, many types search for food in large flocks and sleep at night in large roosts. If you have a parrot or parakeet as a pet, give it foraging toys and puzzle toys to keep it entertained. Spend as much time as you can talking to and playing with your parrot.

Budgerigar

The budgerigar, or budgie, is one of the most popular pet birds in the world. It comes in a countless variety of colors, from green and blue to white and yellow.

Where in the World?

The budgerigar comes from Australia. In the wild, the birds fly around in large flocks. In 1840, the English explorer John Gould took a pair of budgies back to England for breeding. Over time, different color types appeared.

The budgie is usually active and sociable.

20

Breed Profile

The budgie is a type of parakeet, a member of the parrot family. It grows to about 7 inches (18 cm) long. Budgies are mostly apple green and yellow with a bluish tail in the wild. There are many other color varieties in captive birds. The budgie is a good mimic and can be taught to talk. Pet budgies live for 7 to 10 years.

Looking After Me

The budgie does not need a very large cage. It is a good pet bird for people who live in an apartment.

- ☑ It feeds on a special budgerigar seed mix and leafy greens. It also likes carrots and apples.

- ☑ Budgies need exercise outside the cage, but may be reluctant to return!

African Gray Parrot

The African gray parrot is one of the most talented talkers. Highly intelligent and sociable, it is a favorite with bird keepers.

Where in the World?

There are two forms of the African gray—the Congo and the Timneh. The Congo is found across Central Africa, from the west coast to Tanzania and Kenya in the east. The slightly smaller Timneh comes from Ivory Coast and Guinea in West Africa.

The African gray is a smart bird.

Breed Profile

African grays grow to 11 to 13 inches (28 to 33 cm) in length. They have gray plumage with bright red or maroon feathers on the tail. Adults have yellow eyes. Young birds have gray eyes. The African gray is one of the best talkers. It learns new words quickly. These birds can live for 50 to 70 years in captivity.

Looking After Me

African grays are very smart and need lots of activity to keep them from getting bored. Foraging and puzzle toys are good.

 They are curious birds and need plenty of time outside the cage.

 They need a complete pellet diet or seed-based mix, as well as fruit, leafy greens, and vegetables.

Canary

Canaries are prized for their ability to sing. They come in a wide range of colors. Some types have frilled plumage.

The canary is a good pet for people who live in an apartment.

Where in the World?

Canaries come from the Canary Islands, off the northwest coast of Africa. They also live on the Azores and the island of Madeira. The first canaries were taken to Europe in the 1500s. They became popular for their beautiful singing.

Breed Profile

The canary is a member of the finch family. It grows to 4.5 to 8 inches (11.5 to 20 cm) long. In the wild, the canary is a dull brownish green. Domestic canaries vary in color from white and yellow to bright red and orange. They can live for 8 to 10 years.

Looking After Me

Canaries are cheerful, active birds, but they like company and are best kept in pairs.

 Put sand sheets or bird sand at the bottom of the cage to help the canaries digest their food.

 They need a special canary seed mixture, leafy greens, and fruit.

Zebra Finch

The zebra finch is one of the most popular finches. It is easy to care for and is an ideal beginner's pet. It prefers to have a companion.

The zebra finch is a friendly bird but is unlikely to be finger tame.

Where in the World?

Zebra finches live wild in Australia and on some Indonesian islands. The first Europeans in Australia described the birds in 1805. Zebra finches were first bred in captivity in Europe from the middle of the 1800s.

Breed Profile

The zebra finch grows up to 4 inches (10 cm) in length. Females are grayish brown with an orange beak. Males have black-and-white bands on the throat, brown patches with white spots on the body, and orange cheek patches. They can live for five to eight years.

Looking After Me

The zebra finch is a small, active bird that is easy to look after, although it likes to fly and hop about most of the day.

- ✔ Zebra finches don't like to be alone. They are best kept in pairs.

- ✔ They feed on seeds and greens, such as kale and spinach. You can also buy finch mix.

Make It!
Bird Treats

Make these delicious healthy oatmeal treats for your bird. Most birds will love them.

You Will Need:

1 cup (90 g) dry oatmeal

1 egg

Small amount of crumbled eggshell (optional)

2 to 3 tablespoons honey

Vegetable oil for greasing

1 Ask an adult to preheat the oven to 350 °F (180 °C/gas mark 4).

2 Mix the oatmeal and egg together in a bowl.

3 Add a little of the eggshell if using, for extra calcium.

4 Add 2 to 3 tablespoons of honey.

5 Grease a cookie sheet with a little vegetable oil.

6 Spread the oatmeal mixture onto the cookie sheet.

7 Bake the mixture in the oven for 8 to 10 minutes, or until it is firm. Ask an adult to take it out of the oven.

8 Allow to cool, then cut the mixture into small, bite-sized treats.

You can keep any uneaten treats in the fridge for up to three days.

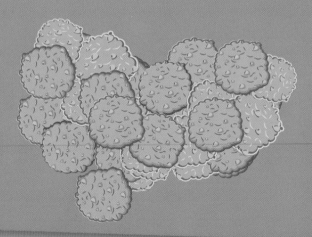

Did You Know?

Puck, a pale blue male budgerigar, knew 1,728 words. Puck even made up his own phrases. He died in 1994, but he still holds the world record for having the largest vocabulary of any bird.

Some birds are so smart they can make and use tools. Crows, for example, use sticks to reach insects in tree bark.

Scientists believe birds developed from therapods, a group of small dinosaurs. The feet of therapods resemble bird feet.

Owls can rotate their heads up to 270 degrees without injuring themselves.

People have used domestic homing pigeons to carry messages for thousands of years. They can find their way home over extremely long distances.

The Christmas Island frigatebird has a wingspan of about 7 feet (2.1 m). It can stay in the air for a week without resting.

There are about 10,000 recognized bird species in the world. Some 13 percent are endangered.

Hummingbirds can hover, fly forward, and fly backward. They beat their wings about 80 times per second.

A person who studies the behavior and habitat of birds is called an ornithologist.

Glossary

avian relating to birds.

aviary enclosure where birds are kept, usually with space for them to fly.

breed (1) to take care of a group of animals to produce more animals of a particular kind. (2) a particular kind of animal that has been produced by breeding.

calcium substance that animals and people need for strong, healthy bones.

captivity the state of being kept in a cage.

cuttlebone bone from a cuttlefish, made of light, chalky material.

domestic living with people.

flock group of birds.

foraging searching for something such as food.

millet type of grass seed used for food.

mimic copy someone's behavior or speech.

nutrient substance that animals and people need to live and grow.

parakeet small parrot.

parasite an animal that lives in or on another animal and gets food from it.

plumage feathers covering a bird's body.

preen use the beak to clean and arrange feathers.

protein substance in some foods that animals and people need to live and grow.

roost place where birds rest or sleep.

softbill type of bird that has a bill suited to feeding on soft foods, such as fruit.

territory an area of land that an animal lives in and defends.

Further Resources

Books

Brown, Lolly.
Canary as Pets: The Ultimate Canary Care Guide, NRB Publishing, 2016.

Gardeski, Christina Mia
Pet Birds: Questions and Answers (Pebble Plus), Capstone Press, 2016.

Thomas, Isabel.
Beaky's Guide to Caring for Your Bird, Heinemann-Raintree, 2015.

Websites

Due to the changing nature of Internet links, PowerKids Press has developed an online list of websites related to the subject of this book. This site is updated regularly. Please use this link to access the list:

www.powerkidslinks.com/cpfk/birds

Birds

Index